Pedal 'n Ponder

Bible quotations are from the New International Version.

To order additional copies, please contact us.
BookSurge, LLC
www.booksurge.com
1-866-308-6235
orders@booksurge.com

Pedal 'n Ponder

A Christian Devotional for Cyclists

John and Marlene Custer

2006

Pedal 'n Ponder

DAY I

Every cycler seems to appreciate the beauty of the ride---the mountains, the lakes, and the trees---and meditates about how it all came into existence. (It is reputed that some bikers only see the white line. Tell me it isn't so.)

It would certainly seem that there has to be a Master Designer to make everything just fit together and relate so well to everything else. I do honestly wonder why the Creator made ants; or why after doing 90 miles, the bees can't leave me alone while I eat my ice cream!

Some would say that molecules just "came together." While I respect their opinion, it is easier for me to believe that a Spirit called *God* actually designed it and made it.

> "In the beginning was the Word [Jesus] and the Word [Jesus] was with God, and the Word [Jesus] was God. He was with God in the beginning. Through him all things were made; without him nothing was made that has been made. In him was life, and that life was the light of men. The light shines in the darkness, but the darkness has not understood it." *John 1:1-5*

We call the Bible *God's Word* and Jesus, *The Word of God.* God is declaring that He made everything! If He didn't, then how can we believe anything the Bible says?

In another passage it says, "all things were created by him [Jesus] and <u>for</u> him [Jesus]." (Col. 1:16) Assume that is true. Why would God create you? You have 90 miles to come up with the answer.

Prayer for the day: "Oh, God, creation is evidence that you exist; help me to believe in you. If you made me *for* you, then help me to know you and understand you better. Amen"

***

DAY 2

Biking through southern Indiana about dusk, with only 5 miles to go, a small animal ran across the road about 15 feet in front of me. I was cruising about 15 mph when I realized it was a skunk. I swerved to the left; then he turned around and headed for my front tire. To keep from hitting him, I instinctively hit the brakes. Then he stopped, turned around again, and, 'instinktively' lifted his tail. I could not get going because I was in a higher gear.

"…all our righteous acts are like filthy rags…" *Isaiah 64:6*

OK. The skunk did not get me that time, but I have finished many a ride smelling as if a skunk DID get me. I've been told to leave my clothes in the garage rather than stink up the whole bedroom.

So why would God say our righteous acts are like filthy rags? Are the good things we do not worth anything? Not when compared to a holy standard---Himself.

So many times we do good things for all the wrong reasons: "it's good for business", "people will think good of us", "it will look good on a resume", or, get this, "I'll think better of myself".

Consider this promise of God for today, "If we walk in the light, as he is in the light, we have fellowship with one another, and the blood of Jesus, his Son, purifies us from all sin." *I John 1:7*

We're only fooling ourselves if we think we are clean inside. We have ALL done things that we are ashamed of, things that we hope no one will ever know about. There is only one way that we can really be clean. A shower at the end of today will only make you clean on the outside!

JOHN AND MARLENE CUSTER

Prayer for today: "Lord, I know that I am dirty on the inside. Forgive me and make me clean. Help me to do what is right. Help me to strive for Your standard. Amen"

***

DAY 3

It was a beautiful summer day. Although the temperature was pleasant at the start, it was predicted to go into the upper 90's in the afternoon. Fifteen miles into the ride we stopped for breakfast. Tom and I got a normal breakfast but Al got only a cinnamon bun. Later we stopped again, but Al only got something to drink.

Later Al complained that the heat was really getting to him. I was surprised because he was a stronger rider than either Tom or me. As we continued to ride, he stopped frequently for rest. Then he said, "John, I can not go any further. The heat got me. Call the SAG."

Then I asked him what he had eaten that day and he told me only the cinnamon bun. It wasn't heat related! Al **bonked!** He had not eaten enough.

> "I [Jesus] am the vine; you are the branches. If a man remains in me and I in him, he will bear much fruit; apart from me you can do nothing." *John 15:5*

In this passage Jesus is saying that we cannot survive spiritually unless we take spiritual nutrition from Him. I'm sure you can name people who are "religious", go to church, or serve on the church board, but their lives are empty----fruitless. Even though they go through the motions, their spirituality is not attractive.

So how do we take spiritual life from Jesus? We must first be "born" into his family by believing in him and asking him to forgive us of our sins and then we must read his word, the Bible, and pray to him. Admittedly, most people feel very self-conscious praying out loud to God. However, you are out in the open on your bike. Try it! I do it all the time…..and God will listen….. I promise.

Where are you today? Are you bearing fruit, or spiritually bonking?

Prayer for today: "Lord, I want to be plugged into the 'real' vine. Fill me with your nutrition. Amen."

***

DAY 4

It was the first day of a bike tour around Nova Scotia. We went to an "uppity-snoot" restaurant and got Bay-of-Fundy scallops----the best food I have ever eaten. The next day I ate Bay-of-Fundy scallops again. I was not disappointed! Later we were to stop at a place that makes ice cream. "It is identifiable because of the flags in the driveway."

It was an 85 mile ride that day and really hot! I couldn't wait for the ice cream near the end of the ride. Certainly a place that makes ice cream would have an air-conditioned parlor to eat it in with nice lounge chairs. It must be nice if they have flags on each side of the drive.........right?

I was riding with the guide when he said, "we're here". Sure enough, there were two little flags by the road.....but this can't be! It was nothing more than a fruit stand where they took orders. They went into the house to fill the orders. (That's also where they made the ice cream.) Meanwhile we dragged lawn chairs to the shade tree. Was I disappointed? Duh!

> "Do not let your hearts be troubled. Trust in God; trust also in me [Jesus]. In my Father's house are many rooms; if it were not so, I would have told you. I am going there to prepare a place for you. And if I go and prepare a place for you, I will come back and take you to be with me that you also may be where I am." *John 14:1-3*

Jesus promised heaven for his family. I don't have room here to print all the scriptures that tell how wonderful it will be. It will be far nicer, however, than any of us can ever imagine! Disappointing like the ice cream stand? No Way!!!

Scripture indicates it will be far more than sitting on clouds playing harps. With resurrected bodies and no sin to mar its beauty, heaven will be far beyond our expectations!

Today's prayer: "Lord, heaven is so distant in my thinking. It is really hard for me to comprehend it. Help me this day to <u>trust</u> that you really are preparing a place for me. Amen."

***

DAY 5

Eric had just graduated from high school and I asked him to go on GOBA (Great Ohio Bicycle Adventure) with me again. Eric was full of fun and it was like reliving my youth just to be around him. Eric did not lack self-esteem! Not at all!

We were on this back road following an attractive girl. Eric decided he was going to show me his charm with girls. He whispered, "watch this, John", then he edged up beside her.

"Hi. My name is Eric." The chatter went on for several minutes. Then, "I'm going to be a freshman at Akron U this fall." "That's nice, Eric. Maybe you'll be in one of my classes. That's where I teach."

I was laughing my head off. Then Eric was riding with me again.

> "Love is patient, love is kind. It does not envy, <u>it does not boast</u>, it is not proud. It is not rude, it is not self-seeking, it is not easily angered, it keeps no record of wrongs. Love does not delight in evil but rejoices with the truth. It always protects, always trusts, always hopes, always perseveres." *I Corinthians 13:4*-7

We've all done a little bragging…..like the first time we did a century. (Certainly that wouldn't be the reason we want to do a cross-country, would it?)

Think today about how that makes the person feel that you are bragging to. Inferior? Inadequate?

Then think about how love relates to boastfulness.

(Do you think about stuff like this more when you are going up a hill, down a hill, or on level ground?…..or none of the above?)

Prayer for the day: "Lord, even when I try, I am often disappointed in my ability to love. I need your help. Amen."

***

DAY 6

Sometimes good rides just happen and other times they are well planned. Well this 70-miler was well planned. I was riding from my home in Wooster, Ohio to my daughter's house in Mt. Vernon. That meant I would be going thru the hills of Holmes County. Holmes County is home to the largest Amish settlement, and it is very beautiful. One of the first things you would probably notice is their unusual dress. (They don't wear the Spandex pants.)

There is something refreshing about their simple life. Notice, I said "simple"....not "easy". Plowing their fields by a team of horses is not as comfortable as riding in an air-conditioned tractor. Riding a bike, likewise, isn't as easy as riding in an air-conditioned car either. So.....maybe we are a new breed of Amish.

Even though I had a map, food, and my wife was going to meet me at the end of the trip, I made a wrong turn. It didn't happen in the flat part of the trip. It happened after I climbed a long hill, which meant I had to re-climb it on another road.

> "Have mercy on me, O God, according to your unfailing love; according to your great compassion blot out my transgressions. Wash away all my iniquity and cleanse me from my sin. For I know my transgressions, and my sin is always before me. Against you, you only, have I sinned and done what is evil in your sight." *Psalms 51:1-4*

The above words were written by King David who messed up! He had sex with another man's wife, had her husband murdered, then married her.

What do you do when you mess up? Justify what you do? Blame someone else? Pretend that you didn't hurt anyone?

David asked God to forgive him and took responsibility for what he did. Even though David was punished for what he did, God forgave him and later God called him, "a man after my own heart" (not because of his sin, but because he worshipped God without reserve.)

Today's prayer: "Lord, help me to truly repent when I fail."

***

DAY 7

I had a seminar in the morning so Al and I couldn't leave until after noon on our four-day ride. I had my pantiers loaded…much too heavy!

We pressed hard to made our first day's destination before dark. It was 80 miles and we got in shortly after dark. Then we cleaned up and got a big spaghetti dinner.

I did not sleep much that night and the next morning it was raining and cold. I was uncomfortable and really tired, so after 25 miles I called my wife to come get me. I had never done that before. I felt bad about it and pondered what went wrong.

> "Therefore, since we are surrounded by such a great cloud of witnesses, let us <u>throw off everything that hinders</u> and the sin that so easily entangles, and let us run with perseverance the race marked out for us. Let us fix our eyes on Jesus, the author and perfecter of our faith, who for the joy set before him endured the cross, scorning its shame, and sat down at the right hand of the throne of God. Consider him who endured such opposition from sinful men, so that you will not grow weary and lose heart." *Hebrews 12:1-3*

What kind of baggage are you carrying that is making life difficult? I'm not talking about what is on (or behind) your bike. I'm talking about lifestyles, unforgiveness, anger, guilt, bitterness, irresponsibility, restlessness, addictions or something else.

Determine right now to get rid of it. Ask God to help you. You may have to ask someone else to help you too….but don't keep carrying it.

13

Prayer for the day: "Lord, you know what I am carrying and how heavy it is. Help me! Help me to know whom I should ask to help me and help me to have the will to follow through. Amen."

Have a good ride!

***

DAY 8

The other day I was on the last third of an 85-miler when I came across a "Detour – Bridge Out". Whether you are on a bike or in a car, we all hate those signs. The incident brought back a memory of years earlier on the same road. I came across the same sign. However, I was then a Funeral Director leading a procession of 25 cars to a rural cemetery. I didn't know the back roads very well so I pulled to the side. A family member came up to my car and said, "John, I work for the County Highway Department. Do you want me to take the lead?"

I know that men don't like to ask for directions, but I was grateful for his offer and followed him to the cemetery.

"Jesus answered, 'I am the way and the truth and the life. No one comes to the Father [God] except through me'". John 14:6

Jesus made many very bold claims. He said he was God's son, that he and his father were one, that there is only one way to know God, and that he is the "way", the "truth" and "life"!!!

Everyone has to decide whether Jesus really was God or the biggest fake this world has ever known. Consider this: all but one of the apostles (disciples) died a martyr, refusing to deny the deity of Jesus. The other one died of old age abandoned to an island for his faith.

Here is the point: if Jesus really is God, (and I believe he is) then he really does know _the way_ and it would behoove us to follow him.

The way to what? The Atlantic? The Pacific? The next town? No, the way through life, the way to God, the way to truth, and the way to eternal life. Notice I haven't said the way to easy street. There will be hills, tar on the road, flats, and breakdowns, but you will have a GPS that will guide you to the destination.

Prayer for the day: "Lord, I'm not used to being told where to go, and I'm having a hard time trusting you. Help me. Amen."

***

DAY 9

As I was putting air in my tires for a day ride, two little girls on their bikes with training wheels pulled into my drive. "Are you going to ride your bike this morning?" one asked. "Yes", I replied. "In fact, I am going to ride my bike all day today." I noticed the quizzical look on her face as she asked, "Does that mean you won't be able to go potty until tonight?"

Isn't it interesting how our concerns change as we grow older? We are first concerned only about eating and keeping dry, then, when we can go potty, then what school to go to, what job to take, who to marry, and then what will go first, ... our knees, ... our brain...........or our wallet.

> "'For I know the plans I have for you', declares the Lord, 'plans to prosper you and not to harm you, plans to give you hope and a future.'" Jeremiah 29:11

Many bikers are riding in hopes of finding a new direction in their life. God says in the above passage that He has **good plans** *for you!* (We know that verse applies to us because it is consistent with His character.)

How do you know what God has planned for you? Start by developing a relationship with God through prayer and let his Holy Spirit abide within you. The Holy Spirit will guide you. I will acknowledge that most people don't seek direction that way, but those who do, find that a relationship with God is most beneficial.

Jesus Christ even mentions the Holy Spirit's "leading" in the "model" prayer that He gave us, *"Lead us* not into temptation." (Matthew 6:13)

I am challenging you today to talk to God (pray). Tell Him exactly what you want, what your concerns are, then wait for His response. He will hear you. He wants a relationship with you.

Prayer for the day: "Lord, you know my concerns." (state them) "I ask your Holy Spirit to indwell me and guide me to a fruitful life. Amen."

***

DAY 10

Psalm 19
The heavens declare the glory of God;
The skies proclaim the work of his hands.
Day after day they pour forth speech;
night after night they display knowledge.
There is no speech or language
Where their voice is not heard.
Their voice goes out into all the earth,
Their words to the ends of the world.
In the heavens he has pitched a tent for the sun,
which is like a bridegroom coming forth from
his pavilion,
like a champion rejoicing to run his course.
It rises at one end of the heavens and makes its circuit to
the other; nothing is hidden from its heat.
The law of the lord is perfect, reviving the soul.
The statutes of the Lord are trustworthy,
making wise the simple.
The precepts of the Lord are right, giving joy to the heart.
The commands of the Lord are radiant,
giving light to the eyes.
The fear of the Lord is pure, enduring forever.
The ordinances of the Lord are sure
and altogether righteous.
They are more precious than gold, than much pure gold;
they are sweeter than honey, than honey from the comb.
By them is your servant warned;
In keeping them there is great reward.
Who can discern his errors?

Forgive my hidden faults.
Keep your servant also from willful sins;
may they not rule over me.
Then will I be blameless, innocent of great transgression.
May the words of my mouth and the meditation of my
heart be pleasing in your sight,
O Lord, my Rock and my Redeemer."

***

DAY II

A 2-1/2 day charity ride left Cleveland for Columbus in the rain, a distance of 225 miles. Six miles into the ride a rider slipped on a bridge and dislocated his shoulder. After they took him to the hospital, I tried to catch the group.

Sue decided to do the ride as a personal challenge. She was not athletic and had a severe diabetic condition. After months of training, overcoming huge obstacles, she felt she was ready.

The first rider that I caught up with was Sue. She was on the side of the road waiting for the SAG---and crying. She said the hills were too much. I encouraged her and told her I would ride with her. I rode with her the rest of the day and she finished the ride with a tremendous sense of accomplishment. Even though I did it, I was very frustrated!

Jesus said, "A man was going down from Jerusalem to Jericho, when he fell into the hands of robbers. They stripped him of his clothes, beat him and went away, leaving him half dead. A priest happened to be going down the same road, and when he saw the man, he passed by on the other side. So too, a Levite, when he came to the place and saw him, passed by on the other side. But a Samaritan, as he traveled, came where the man was; and when he saw him, he took pity on him. He went to him and bandaged his wounds, pouring on oil and wine. Then he put the man on his own donkey, took him to an inn and took care of him. The next day he took out two silver coins and gave them to the innkeeper. 'Look after him,' he said, 'and when I return, I will reimburse you for any extra expense you may have.' Which of these three do you think was a neighbor to the man who fell into the hands of robbers?" *Jesus* Luke 10:30-36

When we are "the good Samaritan", it will require that we inconvenience ourselves. It may cost us time, money, influence, or something else that is precious to us.

Today's prayer: "Lord, give me a heart like yours. Amen."

***

DAY 12

One of the things that I like about biking is that I can sing out loud, pray out loud, and sometimes think out loud. (Cows give me odd looks but I've learned to deal with that.)

What do you think about the most when you are riding: the scenery, the next stop, or something else?

Some of the things we think about are unhealthy. When you dwell on the hurts and abuse that you have experienced, it can be either healthy or unhealthy depending on how you think about it. It is amazing to me how many adults are carrying the baggage of past hurts into their adult life. If you are going to think about those hurts, think of them in a positive way, like trying to understand why the person who hurt you acted that way, or make a decision to forgive the person---even though they are NOT repentant. Forgiveness is the only way to freedom from those experiences. Those are healthy thoughts.

When you visualize yourself in immoral situations---and that is easy to do---it is unhealthy.

> "Blessed is the man who does not walk in the counsel of the wicked or stand in the way of sinners or sit in the seat of mockers. But his delight is in the law of the Lord, and on his law he meditates day and night." Psalms 1:1-2

The Apostle Paul said, "...and we take captive every thought to make it obedient to Christ." II Corinthians 10:5 You **can** control your thoughts!

Let me give you a few ideas: think about how God's Word could apply to your life, think about what you could do to make the world better, or even memorize some Bible verses.

Prayer for the day: "Lord, many of my thoughts are not healthy or wholesome. Help me to think about you, and to think positive, healthy thoughts. Amen."

Sow a thought, reap an act.
Sow an act, reap a habit.
Sow a habit, reap a character.

***

DAY 13

For me, the most difficult commandment that Jesus gave was:

"Love the Lord your God with all your heart and with all your soul and with all your mind and with all your strength." Mark 12:30

I loved my wife and my children. Admittedly, I loved my job, my house and my car----------and of course, my bike! I had to admit, though, that I had questions about my wholehearted love for God. I began reading other Bible passages along with books by Christian authors to find out more about loving God.

I learned that Jesus said in John 14:21:

"Whoever has my commandments and obeys them, he is the one who loves me."

The more I thought and prayed about God's love for me, the more I wanted to follow what He taught. And the more I followed Him, the more I loved Him! I am on a journey; I have not arrived.

In our American culture it is easy to get caught up in material-ism. One thing that I admire about bikers is that you are setting aside some time to ride, think, and appreciate the world that God has made. *That* can be one form of worship and God likes it.

You are on a journey. Keep pedaling! May God's tailwind push you closer to Him.

Prayer for the day: "Lord, I don't always love you the way you commanded. Frankly, my life is often all about *me*. I want to do what you taught with all my heart, soul, mind, and strength. Help me to love you more than anything else. Amen."

***

DAY 14

Riding along a trail several weeks ago I noticed a big raccoon lying by the trail. I've seen them laying by the side of the road after being hit by a car, sometimes with a Gatorade bottle in their mouth---thanks to our fellow bikers! This raccoon, however, was not near a road so I turned around and stopped to look at him closely. It was really hard to tell, but I could see that he was breathing.

That's the way it is with a lot of Christians. You can't tell whether they are spiritually dead or alive. They go to church, say the right things, but their lives don't cut it where the rubber meets the road.

I don't want to be that way! I want to be full of love for God and also for everyone that I come in contact with. I want to overflow with joy and kindness.

> "But the fruit of the Spirit is love, joy, peace, patience, kindness, goodness, faithfulness, gentleness and self-control. Those who belong to Christ Jesus have crucified the sinful nature with its passions and desires. Since we live by the Spirit, let us keep in step with the Spirit. Let us not become conceited, provoking and envying each other." Galatians 5:22-26

This is the model of a good Christian. This is the goal! When we live this way, we will be attractive to others.

Prayer of the day: "Lord, help me to live by *your* standard instead of modeling what I have seen. May I exhibit the fruits of the Spirit in my life...and may I *look* alive! Amen."

***

DAY 15

By Marlene Custer

Probably the thing I enjoy most about riding is being close to nature, and going slow enough to enjoy it. One day while riding along an abandoned canal, I saw a long log stretching across the shallow water. Along the log were 16 – 20 turtles sunning themselves. I had to stop and just observe them for a while.

Often as I ride along a blue jay or a cardinal will dart across the path in front of me. It never becomes common to me. I am awestruck every time. I think of the following scriptures:

> "Look at the birds of the air; they do not sow or reap or store away in barns, and yet your heavenly Father feeds them. Are you not much more valuable than they?"

> "Are not two sparrows sold for a penny? Yet not one of them will fall to the ground apart from the will of your Father......
> So don't be afraid; you are worth more than many sparrows."
> Matthew 6:26, 10:29, 31

I am so glad our Creator did not just create then leave us to fend for ourselves. Not only did He give us Jesus and the Bible, but He knows us and cares about everything that happens to us.

Prayer for today: "Thank you, God, for caring for me. Help me to be aware of your presence today. Amen"

***

DAY 16

When I was just out of college I heard a minister preach on the following passage and it had a big impact on me:

> "Do not store up for yourselves treasures on earth, where moth and rust destroy, and where thieves break in and steal. But store up for yourselves treasures in heaven, where moth and rust do not destroy, and where thieves do not break in and steal. For where your treasure is, there your heart will be also." *Jesus* Matthew 6:19-21

(When you first read these verses, you might get the impression that Jesus was opposed to us owning anything. I really don't think that he was implying that because his closest friends, Mary, Martha and Lazarus, owned a house.)

When I heard the sermon I had just bought my first house, had just bought a fairly new car and already owned a second car. If the trend had continued, I may have spent my life "acquiring" all kinds of things. At that time, I reassessed my priorities and shortly thereafter adopted a Korean daughter. Later we adopted another Korean daughter. My treasure was no longer in things---even though I owned things. Instead my desire was to please my Heavenly Father.

I think Jesus was saying that He wants us to seek HIM, to do His will and he will see that we get what we need. Later in the same chapter, Jesus said, "Seek ye first the kingdom of God and his righteousness and all these things will be added unto you."

So don't feel guilty about your new TREK.....or your new GPS. However, if you put more value on these things than on your relationship with God, then you are on very, very thin ice!

It takes constant vigilance to keep our priorities right.

Prayer for the day: "Lord, help me to prioritize my life in accordance with your will. Amen."

***

DAY 17

I told you about Eric earlier. Some of Eric's friends were letting him draft off of them. One day Eric told me that some man got upset with him. I asked him what happened and he said, "The man I was following said, 'Son, you are drafting off of me!' I told him, 'No, I am not. I am just following you really close.'" I told Eric that it was impolite to draft off of someone without their permission.

Drafting can be a really good thing. We've all benefited by drafting in wind. We can even benefit by drafting off of someone spiritually.

> "You are the light of the world. A city on a hill cannot be hidden. Neither do people light a lamp and put it under a bowl. Instead they put it on its stand, and it gives light to everyone in the house. In the same way, let your light shine before men, that they may see your good deeds and praise your Father in Heaven." *Jesus* Matthew 5:14-16

When you live a consistent life, it makes it easier for others who are watching you to also live a consistent life. The converse is also true. You are influencing others whether you realize it or not. Just think of the people who have told you things like, "You have inspired me to buy a bike and I have started riding it", or "You've caused me to start getting in shape!" Or, "Because of you I have started doing more fun things with my wife."

Remember that if someone is drafting off of you, you have a responsibility to warn them of the potholes in life's road. Maybe it's your son, a fellow worker, or a friend.

Are you taking spiritual responsibility for those drafting off you? I hope you are not someone who would veer for a physical pothole and warn those following you, but totally pretend that a spiritual pothole doesn't even exist.

Prayer for today: "Lord, I am afraid I haven't been as concerned about the spiritual potholes as I should have been. Help me to be more aware of my spiritual safety, and help me be a good example for those following me. Amen"

***

DAY 18

It was a beautiful Fall day and I had just gone through a valley and was starting a climb when I noticed about 20 pure white geese on a grassy area. They were as white as fresh snow and impressively beautiful, so I stopped to look at them more closely. Then I noticed to one side a solitary brown turkey! What a contrast to the beautiful geese. In a weird way, I felt sorry for him. I guess I felt that way because there have been many times in my own life when I felt like the turkey among so many beautiful geese.

> "Now the body [this refers to all believers in Jesus] is not made up of one part but of many. If the foot should say, 'Because I am not a hand, I do not belong to the body,' it would not for that reason cease to be part of the body. And if the ear should say, 'Because I am not an eye, I do not belong to the body,' it would not for that reason cease to be part of the body. If the whole body were an eye, where would the sense of hearing be? If the whole body were an ear, where would the sense of smell be? But in fact God has arranged the parts in the body, every one of them, just as he wanted them to be. If they were all one part, where would the body be? As it is, there are many parts, but one body." I Cor 12:14-20

No matter how many times we have felt rejection by the people around us, God will NEVER reject you when you want to be part of His family!!! He loves you and He made you just the way He wants you to be.

The body of the church needs people of varied gifts and each one is important. I have been an Administrator of a large church and I have also cleaned toilets in a large church. Both jobs are necessary.

Jesus, himself, washed his disciples feet---a very humble position in the Jewish culture.

Prayer for the day: "Lord, Help me not to think of myself as a turkey among the beautiful geese, but rather help me to see myself as you see me. Amen."

***

DAY 19

Some days I don't feel like riding. Maybe it's too hot; maybe it's too cold. For me the ideal temperature is 60°-80°. We have all ridden when the conditions weren't ideal. What biker hasn't ridden in the rain!

We've done other things, too, that were outside our comfort zone: like eat food that we don't like because a job hangs on it---or someone special prepared it.

There is a similar correlation to the spiritual. Many do NOT want anything to do with Jesus Christ because His standards take them out of their comfort zone. They simply avoid anything to do with Him. They don't read His Word, the Bible, they don't pray, they don't go to church, and they even avoid thinking about the consequences of ignoring God!

> "Come to me, all you who are weary and burdened, and I will give you rest." *Jesus* Matthew 11:28

> "…but whoever drinks the water I give him will never thirst. Indeed, the water I give him will become in him a spring of water welling up to eternal life." *Jesus* John 4:14

> "For the Son of Man came to seek and to save what was lost." Luke 19:10

> "Peace I leave with you; my peace I give you. I do not give to you as the world gives. Do not let your hearts be troubled and do not be afraid." *Jesus* John 14:27

I will not tell you that serving Jesus is the easy road, but it is the <u>only</u> way to find true meaning to life and the inner joy that we all crave. I recommend that you think about that.

Prayer for the day: "Lord, so often I take the most comfortable way when it comes to the spiritual. Help me to seek truth. Help me to develop a *personal* relationship with you. I want my life to have meaning! Amen."

✳✳✳

DAY 20

If I ever start a tour company, I'm going to have a trailer on the back of the van with a Porta-A-Pot in the center of it. I'd call my tour group, "Classy Tours". Another thing we really need on a ride is "good" food. There's only so much macaroni-n-cheese and hamburgers that a person can take.

There is a story in the Bible of Jesus teaching along the shores of the Galilee. Five thousand people listened all day. *That should make some of the best politicians jealous!* One of Jesus' disciples thought it would be good to feed them but they could only scrounge up a boy's lunch of five small loaves of bread and two fish.

> "Then Jesus directed them to have all the people sit down in groups on the green grass. So they sat down in groups of hundreds and fifties. Taking the five loaves and the two fish and looking up to heaven, he gave thanks and broke the loaves. Then he gave them to his disciples to set before the people. He also divided the two fish among them all. They all ate and were satisfied, and the disciples picked up twelve basketfuls of broken pieces of bread and fish. The number of the men who had eaten was five thousand." Mk 6: 39-44

The second thing I would like to do on my tour group is sign Jesus up so I'd be sure of having food when I needed it.

Seriously, what do you do with this story? It certainly is outside the realm of normalcy. Several options are to totally disbelieve it, to assume that it got distorted and there were fewer people and more fish, or.........you can believe it.

The problem that many have with believing it is the implications it has on the rest of the Bible and what that dictates about our response to God. Like, if this story is true, there is a good chance that the rest of the Bible is also true. If the Bible is true, then it is important for me to comply to what God expects of me. So what do you think?

Prayer for the day: "Lord, I want to know truth. Help me to accept the truth of your word (the Bible) … all of it. Amen."

***

DAY 21

It was Sunday morning---the day of the big parade. The congregation was moving from its old overcrowded facilities to the new church one mile up the road. The parade was led by the pastor, followed by a tractor-drawn hay wagon, a dozen golf carts, a thousand walkers, then the bike riders of which I was one. I rode next to a little girl with training wheels. (She had a steering problem that complicated the ride.)

Just before the parade started I noticed a lady standing in front of the shuttle bus. The bus driver honked his horn several times but she didn't move. When I tapped her on the shoulder and pointed to the bus, she immediately moved to the side. Then I realized she was deaf. I was reminded of the following verse:

"In them is fulfilled the prophecy of Isaiah: 'You will be ever hearing but never understanding; you will be ever seeing but never perceiving. For this people's heart has become calloused; they hardly hear with their ears, and they have closed their eyes. Otherwise they might see with their eyes, hear with their ears, understand with their hearts and turn, and I would heal them.' But blessed are your eyes because they see, and your ears because they hear. For I tell you the truth, many prophets and righteous men longed to see what you see but did not see it, and to hear what you hear but did not hear it." *Jesus* Matthew 13:14-17

Jesus was talking to people who DID understand.

Could it be that the reason so many do not understand the Bible or can not hear God's "voice" is because they are spiritually deaf? What about you? Are you spiritually deaf? Are you open to hearing

God's voice? You can never hear His voice unless you have faith to believe that He exists.

Today's prayer: "Lord, I am open to your voice. Speak to me this day in some way, maybe through the world that I am riding in, or people that I come in contact with, or through your Holy Spirit. Amen."

***

DAY 22

Usually when I finish a ride with my friends, we sit on my front porch and have a big glass of ice water.........then another......and sometimes my wife, Marlene, will have home-made ice-cream or hot brownies for us. Can you imagine how good that would taste right now?

The psalmist, David, wrote:

"As the deer pants for streams of water,
so my soul pants for you, O God.
My soul thirsts for God, for the living God.
When can I go and meet with God?"
Psalm 42:1

You can think of the many religions as man's attempt to get to God. The Bible, however, is about God's attempt to reach out to man. God said, "Call to me and I will answer you and tell you great and unsearchable things you do not know." Jeremiah 33:3. Again he said, "Here I am! I stand at the door and knock. If anyone hears my voice and opens the door, I will come in and eat with him and he with me." Rev. 3:20. Those promises are laced throughout the entire Bible. God is sincere! He wants a relationship with you and me.

The problem so often is that we don't care. We are so into do-ing everything that is fun that we don't yearn for a relationship with God----a spirit that we cannot see.

I am suggesting that you ---today--- take some time to invite God to reveal Himself to you. Tell Him that you want to know him. We call this praying to God, and *God loves it!*

Prayer for the day: "Lord, I confess that I have not longed for you like the deer longs for water. Forgive me. I ask that you help me to develop that kind of desire for you. Amen."

***

DAY 23

Maps. Can you imagine doing this ride without the help of good maps?! Grocery stores, dangerous areas, camping sites, it's all there! Oh! I can't forget the "Cookie Lady". (She's on the Virginia Adventure Cycling map.)

So if it is difficult to cross the U.S. without a map, it is even more difficult to find our way to eternal life (Heaven) without a map. I have heard so many people say, if I just live a good life, that is all that God expects. However, that is NOT what Jesus said. When Nicodemus came to Him...

> "Jesus declared, 'I tell you the truth, no one can see the kingdom of God unless he is born again.' 'How can a man be born when he is old?' Nicodemus asked. 'Surely he cannot enter a second time into his mother's womb to be born!' Jesus answered, 'I tell you the truth, no one can enter the kingdom of God unless he is born of water and the Spirit. Flesh gives birth to flesh, but the spirit gives birth to spirit." John 3:3-7

You can't get to the ocean by guessing and you can't get to heaven by guessing. You have to go by the map---God's Word, the Bible. Jesus said you must be born into His family. That means you must, 1) repent of your sins, 2) ask Jesus to adopt you into His family, and 3) begin to grow spiritually by reading His Word and praying.

I John 1:9 reassures us that **"if we confess our sins, he [Jesus] is faithful and just and will forgive us our sins and purify us from all unrighteousness."**

There are many good books dealing with spiritual growth. Next time you have a good tailwind that puts you into town ahead of time, stop at a Christian Book Store and look over what they have. I try to always be reading something to stimulate my spiritual growth.

Prayer for the Day: "Lord, your word teaches that I cannot just stumble into heaven. I want to be born into your family and live my life the way you want me to. Amen."

***

DAY 24

I had scheduled a number of rides for our church biking club. Some were all day rides, but this ride was focusing on the children and beginning bikers. We started in Smithville and went four miles to a mini-zoo where they had tigers (formerly owned by Mike Tyson), camels, skunks, wolves, and quite a few other interesting animals. John and Andy, two of the better riders, decided to do an extra fifteen miles.

John was riding and looking at his map. Suddenly, he crashed into Andy. Andy wasn't hurt but John was and wasn't on his bike for the rest of the season. John knew the safety rules, but momentarily lost his concentration.

Spiritually, each one of us can lose our concentration and have a serious accident.

> "Be careful, or your hearts will be weighed down with dissipation, drunkenness and the anxieties of life, and that day will close on you unexpectedly like a trap. For it will come upon all those who live on the face of the whole earth. Be always on the watch, and pray that you may be able to escape all that is about to happen, and that you may be able to stand before the Son of Man." *Jesus* Luke 21:34-36

The first time I rode with clipless pedals, I hit some gravel and forgot to pull my heels out, and down I went into a pile of duck scat. (You may have your own word for it.) It can happen so quickly.

Perhaps you are a person who once had a relationship with Jesus but like the verse above, got caught up with the things of life and soon your relationship was something of the past. Now is the best time to renew your relationship with Him. Why not spend a few minutes today as you ride, telling Him how you feel and asking Him to help you.

Today's prayer: "Lord, distance has come between us and I know you didn't move. Help me to be watchful and get back to where I was and be stronger than I was before. Amen."

***

DAY 25

"For the Son of Man [Jesus] came to seek and to save what was lost." *Jesus* Luke 19:10

When was the last time you lost something? Five minutes ago? Was it your flashlight, the adaptor for your presto valve, or the phone number of a valuable contact?

The above word, "lost", has another meaning. Even Webster's other meaning, "destroyed or ruined physically or morally", is not adequate.

When God made mankind, He made him like Himself. And he made man for fellowship. When Adam and Eve sinned God placed a curse on them and also on the whole earth. No more was the relationship with God what it was before. Mankind was *lost.*

People everywhere are struggling for significance, struggling for pleasure, struggling for education, etc. They don't realize it but they are often struggling to get back what was *lost* in the fall. These things are not wrong in themselves, but they can never replace the relationship that God intended for us to have with Him.

However, that is what makes the above verse so meaningful. Jesus said that He came to find and save that which was *lost*. That includes you and me. He is looking for you! He wants to restore the "lost" relationship. He wants you to be whole, holy, full of joy and fulfilled. Does that sound too good to be true? Trust Him.

Prayer for the day: "Lord, if there is a more meaningful life than the one I am living, I want it. If a relationship with you is what I am missing, continue to speak to my heart so that I may know you. Amen."

***

DAY 26

Do you ever feel lonely? I do. I suppose if we were honest, everyone would admit to feeling lonely now and then. Maybe you feel it when you're doing a solo ride and you see a pack of riders heading toward you---laughing, joking and having a good time. Solitude can be wonderful but loneliness is not.

> As he [Joseph] looked about and saw his brother Benjamin, his own mother's son, he asked, "Is this your youngest brother, the one you told me about?" and he said, "God be gracious to you, my son." Deeply moved at the sight of his brother, Joseph hurried out and looked for a place to weep. He went into his private room and wept there." Genesis 43:29-30

Let me refresh the background of this story. Joseph was the next to the youngest of twelve sons, his father's favorite. His older brothers were jealous of him and sold him as a slave to some people traveling to Egypt, then told their father that he died. In Egypt, Joseph was very responsible but a powerful woman falsely accused him and he went to jail. Years later he was released and became the second most powerful man in all of Egypt. When a famine came, Joseph's family came to Egypt for food. They did not recognize Joseph but he knew who they were and was deeply moved at seeing his younger brother. Imagine the loneliness that Joseph experienced at being away from his family and homeland for many years. He didn't do anything wrong to bring that upon himself.

Many Bible heroes experienced loneliness: Jacob, Elijah, Jeremiah, Nehemiah, Jesus and Paul, to name a few. These were great people in the Bible, so don't think bad of yourself because you are lonely. (Beware, however; when you are lonely you are very vulnerable to making bad decisions!)

Jesus said, "…I am with you always, to the very end of the age." (Matthew 28:20) He wants to be your comforter and friend.

Prayer for today: "Lord, I sincerely ask you to be my friend and companion. Amen."

***

DAY 27

You glance up to see if the telephone poles are leveling out... but they just keep going up. When will this hill ever end? The word "jello" reminds you more of your legs than something you eat. (Goin' through Kentucky? This one's for you!)

What's the mountain in your life that you're having a hard time getting over? A divorce? A custody case? A job loss? A business failure? Yours may be different but we all have them. Like biking a mountain, sometimes you just can't see the end!

> "O Lord, you have searched me and you know me. You know when I sit and when I rise; you perceive my thoughts from afar. You discern my going out and my lying down; you are familiar with all my ways. Before a word is on my tongue you know it completely, O Lord. You hem me in-behind and before; you have laid your hand upon me. Such knowledge is too wonderful for me, <u>too lofty for me to attain</u>." *King David* Psalm 139:1-6

David was reflecting on what he knew about God. It was harder for him to grasp that God was so concerned about him than it is for you to cycle over the biggest mountains.

We can no more comprehend that God knows the details of our life, than to imagine how he made the millions of stars. Think back just a few decades ago. People then could not imagine a small computer chip holding the vast amount of data that it holds. Does that make it easier to understand that He, who created everything, could have ways of recording information about us that we can't yet comprehend?

I am not serving a little God! He is all-powerful! All-knowing! All-present! Unchangeable! And He loves YOU and He loves ME!

Yes! It is very hard for me to comprehend his vastness and His love for me. He is definitely interested in the mountains in your life. He wants you to talk to Him about them. Really!

Prayer for the day: "Lord, because I can't comprehend you, I tend to reject you. Help me to believe that you can help me over the mountains in my life. Amen."

***

DAY 28

You come to a crossroad. Left is off the route 5 miles but you're done for the day; straight 15 is a nice camp on the route, right is a beautiful vista. You decide. (The nice thing about crossroads is that you have choices.)

When I applied for the job I told the owner, don't hire me unless you intend to sell the business to me. It was agreed and for the next five years I worked hard for him and we got along great. My parents moved to the town and bought a home and my parents-in-law moved there and built a new home. After five years I came home from vacation. He called me into his office and told me that while I was gone he got a good offer from someone else and sold the business to them.

I was at a crossroad---actually two crossroads (if that is possible). First I had to make a career choice. I was very discouraged and wanted to change careers. Instead I worked for the new owners for two years then moved and started my own business that I ran successfully until retirement. Secondly, was I going to carry the negative feeling toward him for the rest of my life? In a short time I had become very bitter toward him. I had been hurt big time! I knew, however, that God was not pleased with my attitude, and I did not want to remain that way. So on Christmas Eve I went to his house and asked him to forgive me for my attitude. Then I asked God to forgive me and help me. Lastly, I **chose** to forgive him. It wasn't easy and it wasn't instantaneous but it came. Eventually the anger was all gone.

> "For *if* you forgive men when they sin against you, your heavenly Father will also forgive you. But *if* you do not forgive men their sins, your Father will not forgive your sins." *Jesus* Matthew 6:14, 15

We have all been hurt. However, it is to **your** advantage to forgive. Unforgiveness will eat away at you and make you bitter. You will become a slave to it. At this crossroad in life, if you want real freedom you must choose the path of forgiveness.

Prayer for today: "Father, climbing mountains on a bike is easy compared to forgiving. Help me to forgive. Amen."

***

DAY 29

When the weather gets cold in Ohio, some diehards keep right on biking. Not me! I hop on the stationary. The drawbacks are obvious: boring; poor scenery; and you don't get anywhere. It's like a treadmill: you work like crazy and you get off right where you started!

Sometimes life is like that. We go through the daily grind at work, mow the grass at home, watch Monday night football, etc., but when we look back on the past several years, we might not be satisfied with where we are going. It could be that your bike ride is a step in the right direction. I hope so. If it isn't, consider these suggestions:

1. Do a self-evaluation of where you are with your job, with your finances, with your family, and with God.

2. Perhaps in some areas you are doing very good. Pat yourself on the back.

3. Then make a list of the things that need to change. Meditate and pray about what you should do to make improvements in those areas. After you are sure about what you should do, discuss it with those closest to you for their reactions.

4. Plan the expected changes thoroughly. It's kind of like planning a cross-country.

5. Take action. It might be scary but go for it!

"Trust in the Lord with all your heart and lean not on your own understanding; in all your ways acknowledge him, and he will make your paths straight." Proverbs. 3:5, 6

"Your word is a lamp to my feet and a light for my path." Psalms 119:106

Prayer for today: "Lord, I don't want to 'pedal' and go no place. Help me to make good decisions from now on. Help me to consider your will. Amen."

***

DAY 30

What did you do the last time someone threw something out their window at you, cursed you for being on the road, or intentionally ran close to you just because they don't like cyclers?

Think about why we get angry when people do things like that. Is it that we feel threatened, our rights infringed upon, or the frustration that we can't get them and smash their face in?

I'm fascinated by this verse:

> "But I tell you who hear me; Love your enemies, do good to those who hate you, bless those who curse you, pray for those who mistreat you. If someone strikes you on one cheek, turn to him the other also. If someone takes your cloak, do not stop him from taking your tunic. Give to everyone who asks you, and if anyone takes what belongs to you, do not demand it back. Do to others as you would have them do to you." *Jesus* Luke 6:27-31

Ouch! Admittedly, I am still working on applying this verse to my life.

The problem with many so-called "Christians" is that they pick and choose which teachings of Jesus they will abide by and which ones they won't. They are setting their own standards, and their life is no different from the rest of society. Non-Christians can see through their phoniness and don't want any part of it.

This is only one teaching of Jesus that runs contrary to the norm of society. Can you think of others?

Imagine the results if we really applied this to our life?

Prayer for today: "Lord, I have failed to apply this principal to my life. Help me to see the value of living as you taught. Amen."

***

DAY 31

Cyclist have a lot of time to think---when riding, when eating, and when in camp at the end of the day. I would hope that your thoughts are always wholesome, but frankly, most of us have had thoughts that are not wholesome. Here's God's word:

> "...whatever is true, whatever is noble, whatever is right, whatever is pure, whatever is lovely, whatever is admirable—if anything is excellent or praiseworthy—think about such things." Philippians 4:8

> "You have heard that it was said, 'Do not commit adultery.' But I tell you that anyone who looks at a woman lustfully has already committed adultery with her in his heart." *Jesus* Matthew 6:43, 44

> "But among you there must not be even a hint of sexual immorality, or of any kind of impurity, or of greed, because these are improper for God's holy people. Nor should there be obscenity, foolish talk or coarse joking, which are out of place, but rather thanksgiving. For of this you can be sure: No immoral, impure or greedy person—such a man is an idolater—has any inheritance in the kingdom of Christ and of God. Ephesians 5:3-5

So what do we do with verses like this? Is God obsolete, or would it be better to adjust to His will for us? If we decide to truly live by the Bible, then we will definitely be out of step with our society. Just think of how many in our society are into pornography! They are all out of step with God's will.

A Christian in name only is a sham and unattractive. A *true* Christian will be very different---and will be attractive to a very needy world. What will you be?

Prayer for today: "Lord, you know my thoughts and attitudes. Cleanse me and make me clean. Amen."

***

DAY 32

Climbing a long mountain would have undoubtedly been easier when I was younger, but now it is pure work! Why do we do it? Why is it so satisfying to go over the top? Think of the toughest mountain you ever climbed.

I looked at Mt Washington in New Hampshire and wished I were strong enough to climb it. Once a year they allow cyclists to climb it! What a thrill! (We must be nuts to want to do stuff like that!) To do it though, takes commitment, tenacity, preparation, drive, and hard work!

May I suggest that to become part of God's family only takes a simple prayer of asking for forgiveness. Knowing the heart of God, however, takes commitment, tenacity, preparation, drive, and hard work.

> "And you, my son Solomon, acknowledge the God of your father, and serve him with wholehearted devotion and with a willing mind, for the Lord searches every heart and understands every motive behind the thoughts. If you seek him, he will be found by you; but if you forsake him, he will reject you forever." Jeremiah 28:9

> Seek the Lord while he may be found; call on him while he is near. Let the wicked forsake his way and the evil man his thoughts. Let him turn to the Lord, and he will have mercy on him, and to our God for he will freely pardon. 'For my thoughts are not your thoughts, neither are your ways my ways,' declares the Lord." Isaiah 55: 6-8

You don't climb big mountains half-heartedly and neither do

you find God by going after Him half-heartedly. Over and over throughout the Bible we read that God wants us to <u>pursue</u> Him!

So how fervently have you pursued God? Sunday morning, from 11-12? Sorry, that won't cut it. When you want God, like a drowning man wants air----then you will find Him.

Prayer for today: "Lord, I haven't pursued you like I should. There is a hollow place in my heart for you. Help me to let you fill it. Amen."

***

DAY 33

Several years ago I was cycling around Hilton Head with my brother-in-law. (That meant we started looking for a coffee and pastry shop as soon as we turned out of the driveway.) Hilton Head is comprised of many plantations. Each plantation has a fence around it and a guard at the gate to make sure that no one gets into the plantation without proper authorization.

Some of the plantations have several entrances. I discovered that when I was denied entry at one gate I could sometimes go cruising in at another gate.

Heaven has something in common with Hilton Head: you don't get in without proper credentials! (You can't sneak around to another gate and get in there though.)

> "For it is by grace you have been saved, through faith—and this not from yourselves, it is the gift of God—not by works, so that no one can boast. For we are God's workmanship, created in Christ Jesus to do good works, which God prepared in advance for us to do." Ephesians 2:8-10

If you look at the above verse closely, you will notice that you can NOT buy your way into heaven-----not with money, not with your good looks-----not even with good works! I have met many people who really thought they would get to heaven by attending church regularly (as good as that may be), or giving a large amount to a charity, or even by being nice to the inconsiderate clod next door.

Becoming part of God's family is a **gift**. It is a gift from God to you. The fact that you can have it even though you haven't earned it is called *grace*.

You must believe in Him and believe that he will forgive you of your sins when you repent. We call that *faith*.

Prayer for today: "Lord, I always thought it was by my good works that I could earn my way into heaven. Now I realize that eternal life is a gift for those who trust you. Thank you for your grace. Amen."

***

DAY 34

There are a variety of homes along the cycling paths. Each has its own story. I frequently imagine what the stories are.

Sometimes I imagine what it's like to live there. Is it a home full of joy and laughter, or a dysfunctional home abounding with sorrow and frustration? Did they acquire the house through inheritance or hard work? Would they have a nicer home had it not been for illness or some other misfortune?

Last year, while living in The Philippines, I was told that there are 10,000 people each week that migrate from the provinces to Manila looking for a better life only to find no job, no housing, and little food. Those people usually find scrap lumber, blocks and tin and erect a shack anywhere they can find a piece of vacant ground, even though they do not own it. They called those people squatters.

Several years ago the government covered the old city dump with dirt and said the squatters could live there. That area, called Arenda, is now home to 500,000 people. (Imagine the stench!)

There are 150,000 people in Manila whose only occupation is going through trash to find something that can be sold. When we got ready to leave Manila, some little girls that lived near us brought us presents. When we opened them we found that they were things we had thrown out during the previous year.

"Rejoice in the Lord always. I will say it again: Rejoice! Let your gentleness be evident to all. The Lord is near. Do not be anxious about anything, but in everything, by prayer and petition, __with thanksgiving__, present your requests to God. And the peace of God, which transcends all understanding, will guard your hearts and your minds in Christ Jesus." Phil. 4:4-7

JOHN AND MARLENE CUSTER

We do have much for which to be thankful!! Agree?

Prayer for today: "Lord, I thank you for being so good to me. Help me to know how I can share your blessings with others. Amen"

***

DAY 35

It is healthy to laugh (although not always appropriate); and it is healthy to see the funny side of life.

When I was working as a funeral director years ago, a lady came into the funeral home. As I helped her off with her coat, her wig snagged on my fingernail. Both came off (the coat and the wig---not the fingernail).

Another time I was in the X-Ray Department at the hospital and the staff asked me to take a lady in a wheelchair to the third floor to be admitted. She had a large family that followed along. When we got off of the elevator, I noticed that something appeared to be stuck in the wheel. The son leaned the wheelchair to one side while everyone looked. As I started to pull on what appeared to be wrapped around the wheel, the wheel started spinning. Then I realized I was untangling her bra from the wheel!

Do you want more? I could go on all day! (I usually don't because my wife cuts me off.)

> "A cheerful heart is good medicine, but a crushed spirit dries up the bones." Proverbs 17:22

> "...the joy of the Lord is your strength." Nehemiah 8:10

> "Is any one of you in trouble? He should pray. Is anyone happy? Let him sing songs of praise." James 5:13

God wants you to be full of joy! Sour-faced Christians are unattractive (and far too numerous)!

Spend today thinking about fun times that you have had. If you encounter something today that is irritating, try looking at it from a humorous standpoint. I hope you are still laughing when you zip up your tent tonight!

Prayer for today: "Lord help me to have a joy from deep within. Amen."

***

DAY 36

You're nearing the end of your ride. Congratulations! Has the time gone fast or slow? Let's put it this way: did the last six weeks go faster than the same six weeks of last year? I would suspect that it did.

In fact, you will probably find that the older you get, the faster the time goes! There will be a day when you will look back and think, "I can't believe that life went by so fast!" The Bible has a comment on this:

> "Now listen, you who say, 'Today or tomorrow we will go to this or that city, spend a year there, carry on business and make money.' Why, you do not even know what will happen tomorrow. What is your life? You are a mist that appears for a little while and then vanishes. Instead, you ought to say, 'If it is the Lord's will, we will live and do this or that.'" James 4:13-15

Have you heard old-timers say, "The Lord willin', I'll ..." It is because of the above verse that they say that. Whether or not James intended for this verse to be taken literally or not, I do not know, but he definitely wanted us to not be cocky about our remaining days on earth!

I heard someone say the other day, "You **are today**, the product of how you spent your time in the <u>past</u>. What you **will be**, is based upon what you do <u>today</u>!"

The thought to ponder today is 'how do I want my life to end up?' What do I need to change today in order to make that happen?

Now for the tough one, are your goals more materialistic in nature, or character in nature?

71

Prayer for today: "Lord, I realize that a Godly person will make different decisions from an ungodly person. Help me to be Godly and make righteous choices. Amen."

***

DAY 37

By Marlene Custer

One of the best vacations we have had was with some of our family at Hilton Head, South Carolina. The thing that made it especially fun for us was being able to bike all around the island. Since it is not a very large island we covered the same bike paths a number of times. At least twice or more a day we pedaled past a serene little pond. Finally, on the last evening of our vacation we were driving to a restaurant for a delicious meal. On the way we passed the serene little pond. As I was taking in the beauty of the setting my eye was drawn to the far bank. There was one of the largest alligators I have ever seen soaking up the late afternoon sun. "Wow!" I exclaimed. "How many times did we pedal past here with that dude (and who knows how many more like him) within arm's reach?!"

I was reminded of Jesus talking about the hearts of his listeners.

> "You are like whitewashed tombs, which look beautiful on the outside but on the inside are full of dead men's bones and everything unclean. In the same way, on the outside you appear to people as righteous but on the inside you are full of hypocrisy and wickedness." *Jesus* Matthew 23:27, 28

To other people we can have the appearance of being beautiful and at peace with ourselves, but we can't hide those hidden things forever. At some point the 'alligators' make themselves known. The Apostle Paul also warns in Ist Corinthians 4:5, "(Christ) will bring to light what is hidden in darkness and will expose the motives of men's hearts."

I urge you to not be like the serene pond with hidden alligators lurking within. Through prayer and reading God's word let Christ cleanse you so you are beautiful inside and out.

Today's prayer: "Jesus, I want to be clean on the inside as well as on the outside. Help me to become more like you. Amen"

***

DAY 38

One of my heroes is a man named Harry Holt. (I do admire people other than cyclists!) Harry heard that the Korean-GI babies were rejected by the Korean society, so he adopted eight of the children. Realizing that there were many more orphans left behind, he started an adoption agency that became the largest international adoption agency in the world. Then he went back and built an orphanage for the handicapped that were not adoptable. He did all of this with a weak heart. Harry's heart for people and God, however, was anything but weak!

> "A new command I give you: love one another. As I have loved you, so you must love one another. By this all men will know that you are my disciples, if you love one another." *Jesus* John 13:34, 35

> "For God <u>so loved</u> the world that he gave his one and only Son, that whoever believes in him shall not perish but have eternal life. For God did not send his Son into the world to condemn the world, but to save the world through him." *Jesus* John 3:16, 17

We all know people who do good things---many are not Christian believers. I believe that Jesus, however, is talking about a deeper love.

When a person becomes a believer and repents of his sins, then God's Holy Spirit, takes residence inside that person and that person's nature changes. He takes on the nature of God, which is love. Notice in the passage above that God loved so much that he gave until it cost him greatly! We cannot have God's nature and be unaffected by the needs around us. We cannot have God's nature and hate other people.

We see "Christians" who are not loving, and say, "they are just like everyone else." That's because they are not truly a Christian! God wants us to be different---like himself. That's when life begins to be fun----really fun! Think about it.

Today's prayer: "Lord, it is hard for me to grasp that your spirit can live within me to make me different, but I want it. Amen"

***

DAY 39

As we have chatted together for the last several weeks, I hope the time together has caused you to think about God and has also created in you a desire to become part of God's family. So today is a day of decision. Do you believe that Jesus was who he said he was? Do you believe that the Bible was in fact God's Word to us? Do you believe that God loves you and wants to reconcile yourself to him?

You may feel that to become a follower of Jesus Christ means following a bunch of rules to try and keep God happy. The truth is that He loves you and wants you to experience joy, health, peace and prosperity. You can only do that by knowing Jesus as a friend and Savior.

How can you become part of God's family? It is a matter of simply believing.

> "If you confess with your mouth the Lord Jesus and believe in your heart that God has raised Him from the dead, you will be saved." (Romans 10:9)

If you believe, then pray this prayer: "God, I come to You in the Name of Jesus. I ask You to come into my life. I confess with my mouth that Jesus is my Lord and I believe in my heart that You have raised Him from the dead. I commit to follow You for the rest of my life. I thank You, Father, for adopting me into your family!"

Congratulations! You have made the very best decision you have ever made or ever will make. You may not feel any different, but since you believed, you are forgiven and part of God's family. The next step is to grow in this new relationship with God. The best way to do that is to read your Bible every day so that God can speak to you through it, pray to God, and get involved in a good church so that you can have support and fellowship with other believers.

One final thing.........let me know of your decision. (See the next page for my email address.)

***

DAY 40

I would assume that you are near the end of your ride. You'll be dipping your wheel in the water soon. How was it? Did you have fun?

Now you get to do the reassessments and calculations: what was your average mph, your average miles per day, the average climb per day (if you have a GPS), etc.

Let me encourage you to also reflect on your spiritual life: are you growing closer to God? Do you have a greater desire to "know" God? Are you thinking of activities that you can add or delete from your life that would make you more pleasing to God?

I hope that you will go after God *passionately!* Remember, that no matter what you have been through or what you will go through, God loves you and wants a relationship with you. One of my favorite verses is:

> **"In all thy ways acknowledge Him and He will direct thy path."** Proverbs 3:6

If you have enjoyed reading "Pedal 'n Ponder", drop me a note at: JAMLC2003@yahoo.com Be sure to put "Pedal 'n Ponder" as the subject so that I don't delete it accidentally. If you have a special prayer request, I would like to pray with you about it. If you do not have a Bible, let me know that, too.

John

Made in the USA
Columbia, SC
26 October 2021

47867720R00052